freestyle
BMX TRICKS
flatland and air

Acknowledgments

This book would not have been possible without the enthusiasm and passion of Shaun Jarvis and the Freestyle Now team. They kindly gave me hours of their time throughout the entire process, from initial demonstrations of tricks to being the riders that appear in the marvellous photographs throughout the book. Check out what they are up to on www.FreestyleNow.net.

BMX Freestyle is exhilarating, invigorating and exciting and it takes a special photographer to be able to capture this, but then April Ward (www. aprilwardphotography.com) is a special photographer. Once again she has captured the very essence of what makes this sport a lifelong obsession for the riders. A huge thank you April.

Sean D'Arcy

freestyle
BMX TRICKS
flatland and air

SEAN D'ARCY

TECHNICAL EXPERT: SHAUN JARVIS

A Firefly Book

Published by Firefly Books Ltd. 2011

First printing

Publisher Cataloging-in-Publication Data (U.S.)

D'Arcy, Sean.
   Freestyle BMX tricks : flatland and air / Sean
D'Arcy.
[128] p. : col. photos. ; cm.
Summary: Color, step-by-step photos and
instructions of all major elements of BMX tricks,
from flatland to air tricks. Helpful hints and common
problems are included.
ISBN-13: 978-1-55407-818-9 (pbk.)
ISBN-10: 1-55407-818-0 (pbk.)
1. Bicycle motocross.   2. Stunt cycling I. Title.
796.62 dc22   GV1049.3D3739 2010

**Library and Archives Canada Cataloguing in
Publication**

D'Arcy, Sean
   Freestyle BMX tricks : flatland and air / Sean
D'Arcy.
ISBN-13: 978-1-55407-818-9
ISBN-10: 1-55407-818-0
   1. BMX bikes. 2. Stunt cycling. 3. Bicycle
motocross. I. Title.
GV1049.3.D37 2011   796.6'2   C2010-905925-5

Published in the United States by
Firefly Books (U.S.) Inc.
P.O. Box 1338, Ellicott Station
Buffalo, New York 14205

Published in Canada by
Firefly Books Ltd.
66 Leek Crescent
Richmond Hill, Ontario L4B 1H1

Printed and bound in China by South
China Printing Co.

Developed by A&C Black
Cover design, text design and
typesetting by James Watson
Cover photograph © shutterstock.com
Inside photographs © April Ward

Note: It is always the responsibility of the
individual to assess his or her own fitness
capability before participating in any training
activity. Whilst every effort has been made
to ensure the content of this book is as
technically accurate as possible, neither
the author nor the publishers can accept
responsibility for any injury or loss sustained
as a result of the use of this material.

CONTENTS

Introduction

BMX stands for Bicycle Motocross and it was started in the 1960s by kids in California who didn't have the means to buy a motorbike, but wanted to race like Motocross. By the 1970s manufacturers were producing bikes specifically for BMX and the first professional race was held in 1975.

As the sport of BMX racing grew there began an underground movement of BMX Freestyle as riders began to enter skate parks and copy the tricks being done by skateboarders. Riders soon realized that they didn't even need a skate park to do tricks and BMX Flatland was born.

By the end of the 1970s the first professional BMX Freestyle teams began to form and toured the US doing shows. In the early 1980s the first BMX Freestyle competitions were organized and the sport began to explode across the world. Now BMX Freestyle offers a professional career for any rider who has what it takes to go all the way.

Freestyle BMX Tricks has been divided into two chapters: Flatland and Air. Flatland is the art of riding your bike on a flat surface. There are no rules and no limits. Air is when you make your BMX fly and the normal laws of gravity don't seem to apply to you.

This book shows you step-by-step how to do all the tricks needed to be a top freestyler. The rest is up to you – have you got what it takes? Let's get freestyling.

01

Flatland

Flatland is the art of riding your bike on a flat surface. Anything goes, as long as you do it with style, grace and of course you don't fall off.

PUPPET STAND

This is a great trick for a beginner because not only does it look good, but it also helps a rider develop a feel for how to balance the bike.

Starting Position

Move the bike forward at a steady pace, standing on both pedals with the left pedal down.

Step 1

Lift your right leg over the frame.

Step 2

Hop your left foot off and put your right foot on the left pedal.

Shaun's Tip ««

In Step 2, standing up straight will help you balance.

Step 3

Let go of the handlebars and lift your arms up and left leg out.

Remix

Once you have mastered the Puppet Stand then an amazing remix is in Step 1 to put your right foot on the left back peg instead and balance the bike by leaning against the saddle. Much harder, but definitely worth trying.

Secret

You must keep your right leg strong and straight otherwise you will overbalance.

Common Problem

I always fall to my left before I get to let go of the handlebars.

You are pushing down too hard on the pedal in Step 2, which causes your right knee to bend and so you fall over.

ENDO

An Endo is special because not only does it look good, but it really feels good to know you have pushed the bike right to the edge before you overbalance.

Starting Position
Move forward with the pedals level and hands on handlebars.

Step 1
Pull the front brake on.

Step 2

Shift your weight forward and push the handlebars forward.

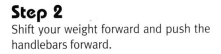

Shaun's Tip «

Lock your arms forward in Step 2.

Step 3

The back wheel lifts off the ground and you balance on the front wheel before letting the back wheel drop down again and roll backward.

Remix

The Endo is perfect all on its own, but a sensational remix is to rock the bike. Straight after the Endo pull the back brake and lift up the front wheel to get that rocking motion going.

Secret

You do not need any speed to do this – everything happens because you shift your weight forward.

Common Problem

I always go over the handlebars.

This is part of learning the Endo. You are going too fast and so your momentum is pushing you over. Just slow down – you don't need the speed.

BUNNY HOP

A Bunny Hop is what you use to make the bike jump and you need to be able to do this to do so many tricks, especially in the Air chapter.

Starting Position

Coast forward standing on the pedals with the pedals level.

Step 1

Crouch down bending your legs and arms.

Step 2

Lift the handlebars up as you stand up straight, which gets the front wheel off the ground.

Common Problem

My wrists always hurt after I have been practicing Bunny Hops.

Your front wheel is landing first so you are taking a lot of impact in your wrists. Just make sure your back wheel touches down first and you will be OK.

Step 3

Push back against the pedals and lift the back wheel up too.

Remix

Most people won't understand how you made the bike leap off the ground in the first place, but a stunning remix is to do it going backward. That will confuse them even more.

Secret

To lift the back wheel you need to have your toes pointing downwards on the pedals, so you can push back against the pedal and lift at the same time.

Shaun's Tip «

Practice lifting the front wheel and the back wheel separately before trying to put the two together in a Bunny Hop.

BACKWARD RIDING

This never fails to get a reaction because it just looks like you shouldn't be able to do it. Again this move is all about balance.

Starting Position

Coast the bike forward at a medium pace with right pedal down and your left foot off the left pedal.

Step 1

Swing your left leg over the frame and on to the right pedal.

Step 2

Move your right foot to the back right peg, then twist it over the saddle to the back left peg.

Shaun's Tip «

Learn how to balance first. Practice coasting backward with one foot on the ground and one on a pedal.

Common Problem

I can ride backward, but not for very long.

You only sit on the handlebars in Step 3 until you switch hands – after that you need to lift off the handlebars so you can use them for balance.

Step 3

Now twist your upper body around and sit on the handlebars, and switch hands on the handlebars.

Remix

A top quality remix is, when riding backward, stand with one foot on the frame of the bike and put the other leg out over the handlebars. It looks killer.

Secret

In Step 3 don't take both hands off the handlebars at the same time. Bring one hand over to the other and only let go of the handlebar just before the other hand grabs it.

TAIL WHIP

This trick just blew Shaun away when he first saw it and it took him ages to perfect it, but he was so stoked when he did. Although it was over 20 years ago now he still smiles at the memory.

Starting Position

Coast forward at a slow pace with both legs on the left hand side of the bike. Your left foot is on the left pedal and right foot in the air above it.

Step 1

Stop the front wheel by quickly pressing the sole of your right foot against it.

Shaun's Tip ◄◄

As the seat swings past the handlebars press the back brake. This stops the right pedal in the best place for you when you have finished the Tail Whip.

Step 2

Shift your body weight forward over the front pegs and lift the back wheel off the ground.

Common Problem

The back end always hits the ground in front of me and never does a full 360.

You are leaning too far forward. You need to keep your body weight over the front pegs. Try pulling the handlebars back towards you as the back end swings around the front.

Step 3

Using your left foot kick the frame of the bike around 360 degrees. Stop the frame with your left foot when it comes around and put your feet back on the pedals.

Remix

If you want to double the wow factor in Step 3, when you stop the frame lean forward again to keep the back wheel up and swing the frame back again 360 degrees. Most people cannot believe a Tail Whip is possible, so a Double Tail Whip has them speechless.

Secret

Have your left foot on the very edge of the left pedal at the start so it is much easier to kick the frame sideways 360 degrees.

MANUAL

The classic trick that just about everybody who has ever ridden a bike has tried to do. Pop the front wheel up and ride.

Starting Position

Coast forward at a medium pace with the pedals level.

Step 1

Lean your body weight backward behind the saddle.

Step 2

Pull the handlebars up towards you to lift the front wheel off the ground.

Shaun's Tip

Learn how to balance on the back wheel first. You can do this by leaning against a wall with the back brake on so you get a feeling for the position your body needs to be in.

Step 3

Coast forward on the back wheel.

Remix

An awesome looking remix is to do the Manual from the back pegs. Everything is the same, but you don't have to pull the handlebars up so hard this time.

Secret

The lower the front wheel is to the ground, the further you have to lean back to keep the Manual going.

Common Problem

I always pull up too hard and loop out.

Just tap the back brake if you feel you are going to loop out and that will bring the front wheel down a bit for you.

FORWARD HANG 5

A big regret for Shaun with the Forward Hang 5 is that he never took the time to learn it over 20 years ago when he first saw it. He cannot explain why he didn't but he wishes he had.

Starting Position

Coast forward at a medium pace with your feet on the pedals.

Step 1

Put your left foot on the front left peg.

Step 2
Lift your right foot off the right pedal.

Shaun's Tip «
Practice balancing on the front wheel first. Using a street curb have your left foot on the left peg, the back wheel in the air and try to balance the bike as you coast forward with your right foot on the curb.

Step 3

Lunge your weight forward and push the handlebars forward – this lifts the back wheel off the ground. Balance the bike on the front wheel.

Remix

A stunning remix of the Hang 5 is to balance with both feet on both front pegs in Step 3. It looks fantastic, although it is harder to keep your balance.

Secret

To help with your balance in Step 3 hold your right foot out to the side away from the bike.

Common Problem

I always overshoot and go over the handlebars.

You have your weight too far forward. Remember your weight should be over the front pegs to get the balance.

FUNKY CHICKEN

When Shaun was younger all his friends would compete against each other to see who could do the longest Funky Chicken. He hasn't told me who used to win.

Starting Position

With the handlebars twisted around stand over the front wheel with your left foot on the front left peg.

Step 1

Grab hold of the saddle with your right hand.

Step 2

Lift your right foot over the handlebars.

Shaun's Tip

Learn to "scuff" first. "Scuffing" is when you spin the wheels of the bike using the sole of your foot.

Step 3

Lift the saddle up and balance the bike on its front wheel. To keep the bike moving "scuff" the front wheel using your right foot.

Remix

An awesome remix is to alter the starting position by standing over the front wheel with the handlebars twisted, but with your left foot on the right front peg. Just that slight change makes everything look entirely different.

Secret

The best way to control your "scuffing" speed is to push the front wheel forward then drag the sole of your foot back along the wheel before pushing forward again.

Common Problem

I always fall backward in Step 3.

As you "scuff" you are not keeping your body weight over the pegs. Try doing smaller "scuffs" but enough to keep you moving.

FIRE HYDRANT

Shaun was out riding with some buddies a few years ago when he met up with some fire fighters who invited them back to the station. Shaun got to do Fire Hydrants at a Fire Station which is pretty cool.

Starting Position

Right foot on left back peg and left foot on left front peg coasting along at a medium pace.

Step 1

Spin the handlebars around 270 degrees keeping your left foot on the peg.

Shaun's Tip «

In Step 1 swing your right leg behind you to keep the handlebars at 270 degrees.

Step 2

Lean back and lift the back wheel off the ground.

Common Problem

Most times when I try a Fire Hydrant I cannot get past Step 1.

You are spinning the handlebars around too fast and so you over-balance. Keep your hips close to the handlebars.

Step 3

The frame of the bike swings around. Stop the frame with your right foot and put your feet back on the pedals.

Remix

As this is a classic linking trick there are many, many great remixes. Shaun's favorite remix is to change the starting position to have your left foot on the left pedal and right foot on the front left peg.

Secret

If you have brakes then pull the front brake as the frame is spinning around to keep the front wheel still.

BOOMERANG

Easy to see where the name came from, but not so easy to do. Follow these steps though and you will be doing it in no time.

Starting Position

Start with both feet on the back pegs and your hands on the handlebars.

Step 1

Swing your right foot out in front and then behind, as you hop off your left foot and begin to swing around the handlebars.

Step 2

Keep your body weight over the handlebars and allow your legs to swing completely around and back towards the back wheel.

Common Problem

I always bail out of the trick in front of the bike.

You could be swinging out too much and so your body weight isn't over the handlebars which is dropping you in front of the bike.

Step 3

When you come around the other side get your right foot back on to the back right peg and you have just done a Boomerang.

Remix

The Boomerang is just a sensational looking trick, but to make it even better start from the pedals and land back on the pedals. Its hard to improve on something this good, but pedal to pedal does.

Secret

Keep your arms straight so it is easier to support your body weight when you swing around the front of the bike.

Shaun's Tip <<

As the handlebars turn 90 degrees, clip on your front brake and release as you go past 180.

DECADE

Quite simply a guaranteed crowd-pleaser – it looks to a non-freestyler that you have just jumped off your bike, but somehow you are still riding it.

Starting Position

Start with both hands on the handlebars with your left foot on the left back peg and your right foot on the frame.

Step 1

Clip the back brake on and lift the front wheel up.

Step 2

Swing your left leg over the raised handlebars and hop off your right foot. Keep your body weight over the bike and swing around the handlebars.

Common Problem

I always land away from the bike.

In Step 2 you are jumping off the bike, instead of over the bike which will allow you to swing back to land the Decade.

Step 3

Land your left foot back down on the frame and your right foot on the right pedal.

Remix

A stunning remix of the Decade is to start with both feet on the back pegs and land on the frame. Another remix is to start and finish on the back pegs. Both of them are rad.

Secret

The higher you lift the front wheel the easier the Decade is to do, so you could do an Endo before you start to give you more momentum and get that front wheel higher.

Shaun's Tip

Position the right pedal about three quarters up so that when you land in Step 3 it's there for you.

HALFHIKER

Done by a quality FlatLander this has to be one of the smoothest looking tricks possible.

Starting Position

Coast forward at a slow pace with both legs on the left hand side of the frame. Your left foot is on the front left peg and your right foot is on the back left peg.

Step 1

Lunge your weight forward and push the handlebars forward to lift the back wheel off the ground.

Shaun's Tip «

Best to get your Hang 5 locked before trying this one.

Step 2

Grab the saddle with your right hand.

Step 3

Place your right foot on the front right peg and glide along balancing on the front wheel.

Remix

This superb remix to the HalfHiker is called the HitchHiker and is actually more popular at the moment. Do all the steps the same, but add an extra step by letting go of the saddle in Step 3 and grabbing the back wheel. HalfHiker just got better.

Secret

In Step 3 hold the frame of the bike slightly to the side so you can move it to help with your balance.

Common Problem

I can never glide along doing the HalfHiker, I always lose it.

Check you have your left hand up to help with your balance and the frame slightly to the side so you can adjust its position.

WHIPLASH

You could call this a moving Tail Whip. Whatever you call it, you have got to learn it.

Starting Position

Coast forward at a medium pace with both legs on the left hand side of the frame. Your left foot is on the front left peg and your right foot is on the back left peg.

Step 1

Lunge your weight forward and push the handlebars forward to lift the back wheel off the ground. Using your right leg push the frame of the bike away from you.

Step 2

Place your right foot on the front right peg and lift your left foot up.

Step 3

Wait for the frame of the bike to come around and catch it with your left foot.

Remix

Just a fantastic remix of the Whiplash is to do it rolling backward. It uses all the same steps, but going backward just adds that extra kick to a great trick.

Secret

Do Step 2 as early as possible.

Shaun's Tip «

Crouch down in Step 1 to help you get the back wheel off the ground when you lunge forward.

Common Problem

I always drop off the front of the bike as the frame spins around.

You have to keep your weight over the handlebars. Try to keep your hips closer to the handlebars and this problem will go away.

TIME MACHINE

This is as close as you can get to doing ballet on a bike. It just looks so graceful.

Starting Position

Coasting forward slowly with your feet on the back pegs and hands on the handlebars.

Step 1

Lift the handlebars up and switch your right hand over to the left grip and take your right foot off the back right peg.

Step 2
Lift your right leg over the saddle to the left side of the frame and grab the front left peg with your left hand.

Shaun's Tip ‹‹
This trick should be done smoothly, so do all the steps in a fluid motion.

Step 3

The bike will begin to pirouette quickly. Let go of the front peg and as the front wheel drops to the ground place your right foot on front left peg.

Remix

A very subtle remix: in Step 1 when you lift the handlebars up, twist them and let go with your left hand so that your right hand is on the left hand side of the frame. It makes the Time Machine flow even more smoothly.

Secret

Bring your right knee up to your chest when the bike starts to pirouette and you will spin quicker and longer.

Common Problem

I always loop out before I even get close to starting the trick.

You are simply jerking up the handlebars too quickly and making it too difficult to balance.

DEATH TRUCK

Fantastic name for a fantastic trick.

Starting Position

Coasting along forward slowly with the handlebars twisted around. Have both feet on the back pegs and your hands on the handlebars.

Step 1

Lift the front wheel up and then let go with your left hand and twist the front wheel 90 degrees with your right hand.

Shaun's Tip ‹‹

In the Starting Position have your right hand in an underhand grip – this makes Step 1 much easier.

Step 2

Reach under the front wheel with your left hand to grab the front peg.

Step 3

Pull the front peg up and towards you, twist the handlebars 180 degrees in between your legs and balance on the back pegs.

Remix

You need to have confidence in your ability to balance for this remix. After you have done Step 3 squeeze your legs together, let go of the front peg with your left hand and do a No-Hander Death Truck.

Secret

Practice balancing the bike in Step 1 first, so that you can do that easily before attempting Steps 2 and 3.

Common Problem

I can never get the handlebars to go between my legs in Step 3.

You really need to have the handlebars up closer to your chest before you try Steps 2 and 3 so they twist through your legs.

INFINITY ROLL

This is called the Infinity Roll, because you can keep rolling in circles until you feel sick or get bored, whichever comes first.

Starting Position

Coasting forward slowly with feet on the back pegs and hands on the handlebars.

Step 1

Do an Endo to get the bike to roll backward.

Step 2

Twist the handlebars to your left by about 75 degrees.

Shaun's Tip

Keep your weight on your handlebars – this will keep them locked at that angle.

Common Problem

I always fall into an Infinity Roll.

Remember: you lean in, but you still need to stay balanced.

Step 3

Put your right foot on the back wheel and drag it down to keep the bike rolling backward in the Infinity Roll.

Remix

A top remix is to go for a Spin Infinity – twist the handlebars 90 degrees in Step 2, with your left hand on the handlebars and right hand on the seat in Step 3. You'll go into a really tight spin. Impressive, but more likely to make you feel sick quicker.

Secret

Push the frame of the bike so it is against your left knee as you lean in to the Infinity Roll.

SPIDERMAN

Pretty easy to see how this trick got its name.

Starting Position

Roll straight towards a wall with your left leg out in front of the left pedal.

Step 1

Click both brakes and swing your left foot behind as you hop off your right foot and begin to swing around the handlebars.

Step 2

Jam your feet against the wall and then climb up it.

Step 3

Climb down and put one foot on the front wheel, then twist the handlebars and climb back on to the bike.

Remix

This remix is to impress your friends. In Step 2 gradually release the brakes until you can form a bridge against the wall and get your friends to ride under you. Absolutely rad.

Secret

You must jam your feet against the wall higher than the handlebars or it becomes very difficult.

Shaun's Tip ◄◄

Don't go too close or too far away from the wall. Stop about the width of the front wheel away.

Air

Air is when you break the laws of gravity and get your bike to fly.

FAKEY

Great riders make this look simple, but that is why they are great riders. It's a terrific trick which will help you land much harder tricks later in the chapter.

Step 1

Approach the ramp straight on with enough speed for the front wheel to reach the coping.

Shaun's Tip

Coast up the ramp in Step 1 and keep the pedals level.

Step 2

As you approach the top of the ramp do a bunny hop.

Common Problem

When I land I always flip out.

You are leaning away from the bike when you land. Try to keep your body over the center of the bike.

Step 3

Land the bike straight and roll back down the ramp Fakey (backward).

Remix

A Fakey allows you to do anything you want while the bike is in the air. Later on you will learn how to do a Bar Spin, TurnDown and TableTop which can all be done while the bike is in the air – too many remixes to mention.

Secret

Practice just rolling back down the ramp without Step 2 first so that you can do Step 3 easily before you put all the steps together.

JUMP

Every rider wants to learn how to jump and then how to jump higher and longer.

Step 1

Approach the ramp with enough speed to go over the coping.

Step 2

As the front wheel goes over the coping do a Bunny Hop.

Shaun's Tip

Learn to Bunny Hop first.

Step 3

Keep the handlebars and bike straight and land back wheel first. You have just done your first jump.

Remix

Almost every trick that follows in this chapter is a remix of a Jump so read on and be amazed at what you can do now you have learned how to Jump.

Secret

Everything is in the Bunny Hop and this will give you more height and a better landing.

Common Problem

I always loop out with the back wheel just sliding under.

I hate to say this, but it is back to the Bunny Hop again. You need to really pick the back end up to stop this happening. Get your Bunny Hops locked and you will be OK.

AERIAL

Shaun first saw an Aerial when the Bob Haro Tour came to town back in 1984 and it just blew him away.

Step 1

Approach the ramp at a slight angle at a moderately fast speed.

Step 2
Before you reach the top begin to turn the handlebars, then do a Bunny Hop.

Step 3

Use your hips to swing the back wheel around and land facing back down the ramp.

Remix

An Aerial is a beautifully graceful trick, but if you plan on becoming a top freestyler then it is essential you can Aerial both to the left and the right off a ramp. So get practicing.

Secret

The higher you go, the easier an Aerial becomes, but higher is scarier.

Common Problem

My bike wheel always hits the ramp and I slide out.

Simple. Increase your approach angle or do a bigger Bunny Hop.

360

A 360 is like ballet on a bike – you float off silently in your own world then the sound of the bike landing brings you back to the wonderful world of BMX freestyle.

Step 1

Approach the ramp straight on, but just before your front wheel goes over the coping twist the handlebars to begin rotating the bike and jump.

Step 2

Twist your upper body and look as far behind you as you can.

Common Problem

I always seem to clip my back wheel on the coping.

You are twisting the handlebars too early, so the back wheel isn't clear of the coping as the bike rotates. Just relax and twist the handlebars higher up the ramp.

Step 3

At 180 into the spin, spot where you want to land, then land with both wheels hitting the ground at the same time.

Remix

A spectacular remix is to land the 360 on a deck just on the back wheel and balance. This remix allows for a graceful landing which suits the trick.

Secret

Throw your head back over your shoulder in Step 2 when you twist your upper body, as this is the key to the 360.

Shaun's Tip

You don't have to go fast or really high to do a 360.

TAIL TAP

Shaun learned how to Tail Tap so long ago that he had to learn it on a street curb as there were no skate parks around.

Step 1

Approach the ramp straight on, but just before your front wheel goes over the coping twist the handlebars and jump.

Shaun's Tip «

Before you land in Step 2 put your brakes on to hold you in that position. The timing is important – don't put the brake on until the back wheel is in the air.

Step 2

When the bike is airborne use your hips to twist the back wheel around, and land on the back wheel at 90 to the ramp.

Common Problem

Whenever I land on the back wheel the front one goes straight down too.

You need to shift your weight back a bit and pull the handlebars up to stop the front wheel dropping in Step 2.

Step 3

Leaning over the ramp, twist the front of the bike so the front wheel goes straight back down the ramp.

Remix

This is a superb remix of the Tail Tap. Between Steps 1 and 2 move your feet from the pedals to be on the back pegs when you land, then step back on the pedals before you go back down the ramp. It looks amazing.

Secret

When you land in Step 2 have the front wheel hanging over the coping.

X-UP

When Shaun was a kid he saw a photo in a magazine of a guy doing an X-Up – it just oozed so much energy and style that he has never forgotten how much it inspired him to learn this trick.

Step 1

Approach the ramp straight on with enough speed to get some air.

Step 2
Twist the handlebars 180 degrees.

Shaun's Tip «
You have to make sure you can get your knees out of the way before you twist the handlebars in Step 2. You can either lean back or open your knees out – whatever works for you.

Step 3

Twist the handlebars back 180 degrees to normal and land the bike.

Remix

A crazy remix is to forget about Step 3 and land the bike with the handlebars twisted. It looks insane but it works.

Secret

To stop your arms locking when you twist 180 in Step 2, maybe loosen your fingers and only hold the outside grip with your thumb and finger.

Common Problem

The back end always flips out when I do an X-Up.

Remember, only the handlebars twist. You are twisting your shoulders and hips which flicks the back end around. You could twist the handlebars the other way.

KICK TURN

The Kick Turn is a retro favorite of Shaun's from way back, and he feels it is only a matter of time before it makes a massive comeback. It just looks so relaxed and cool.

Step 1

Approach the ramp straight on at a moderate pace with just enough speed to go over the coping.

Shaun's Tip

When learning the Kick Turn don't worry about pivoting the bike the full 180 as you can work up to that. Just pivot enough to go back down the ramp.

Step 2

Lift the handlebars up and put the back brake on.

Common Problem

I always loop out when I try it.

It sounds as if you are lifting it too high. Just get it off the ground and then turn down the ramp.

Step 3

Twist your head and upper body around to pivot the bike 180 degrees. Release the brake and ride down the ramp.

Remix

You can do many, many fabulous remixes from a Kick Turn, but the best of them is Kick Turn X-Up. It has the lot, with the back wheel slowly rotating and the front wheel twisting and pivoting. Killer.

Secret

The most important part is to twist your head and look behind you at where you want the front wheel to land.

DOUBLE PEG STALL

The strange thing is Shaun learned how to do a Double Peg Grind before he learned how to Double Peg Stall which means he learned the harder remix first.

Step 1

Approach the ramp straight on with enough speed to reach the coping with your back wheel.

Step 2

Just before the front wheels reach the coping, twist the handlebars though 90 and do a Bunny Hop. Twist your hips to turn the frame around and land the pegs over the coping.

Common Problem

I always bail over the coping when I land.

Your body weight is continuing forward when you land. In Step 2 try leaning back over the ramp more and pushing the bike at the coping to click the pegs into place.

Step 3

Balance on the pegs, then twist the handlebars down the ramp and Bunny Hop off the coping.

Remix

A totally rad remix is a Double Peg Grind. Instead of coming up the ramp straight on, you come up at an angle so you can slide along on the coping when you land the pegs. Cool and lots of fun.

Secret

When you land in Step 2 try to keep your body weight over the ramp and push the bike away from you into the coping.

Shaun's Tip «

Perfect the landing first, then worry about balancing it in Step 3. At the start you could put your foot down until you have the landing locked.

FEEBLE GRIND

This is a trick that originated in Skate, but has now made the crossover to BMX. Just like in Skate, if you hit a Feeble properly you can grind along for as long as there is something to grind on.

Step 1

Approach the ledge almost parallel at a medium pace.

Step 2

Bunny Hop up and twist the frame so that the front wheel lands on the ledge and the back peg grinds on it.

Shaun's Tip ‹‹

Keep your front wheel parallel with the edge of what you are grinding on to lock you into the grind.

Step 3

Bunny Hop off the ledge and turn the handlebars away from it.

Remix

An outstanding remix for the Feeble is the Smith Grind. All the steps are similar but this time the back wheel is on the ledge and you grind on the front peg. Again, hit it fast enough and you grind forever.

Secret

Lean into the ledge to keep the back peg from sliding off and ruining the grind.

Common Problem

My back peg always drops off.

Lean into the ledge to stop this. Use the front wheel as a guide and center your body weight as if the saddle is in line with it.

NOSEPICK

Not a great name for a trick that looks as cool and stylish as this one, but you can see where it comes from. The other name for this trick is FootJam which isn't any better.

Step 1

Approach the ramp straight on, but just before your front wheel goes over the coping twist the handlebars slightly and jump.

Step 2

Bring your weight forward and push down on the handlebars to land and balance on the front wheel. As soon as you land push your foot down on the front wheel like a brake.

Shaun's Tip

In Step 2 land the front wheel at 90 degrees to the ramp and have all your body weight inside the coping.

Common Problem

My back wheel always goes down in Step 2.

Simple: you are over-rotating the bike. You could be twisting your hips as this will usually lead to the back wheel dropping.

Step 3

Take your foot off, pull the handlebars up and Bunny Hop to go back down the ramp.

Remix

A sensational remix to a NosePick is to switch feet in Step 2. First brake the front wheel with your right foot, then switch to jamming with your left, then do Step 3. It just lets everyone know you have total control over your bike.

Secret

Just twist the handlebars slightly in Step 1 and don't try to throw your body weight or twist your hips to get the frame to swing around.

ICEPICK

Shaun has no idea why, but he learned how to do an IcePick in 30 minutes and since then has not done them much at all.

Step 1

Approach the ramp straight on, but just before your front wheel goes over the coping twist the handlebars slightly.

Step 2

With the front wheel in the air, land the back peg on the coping and balance there.

Shaun's Tip «

Keep your knees bent and your weight over the back wheel to keep the front wheel up in Step 2.

Common Problem

I always put my foot down in Step 2.

You still have forward momentum when the back peg lands on the coping. You are either twisting your hips or twisting the handlebars too much in Step 1.

Step 3

Bunny Hop the back peg off the coping, rotate the bike and go down the ramp.

Remix

A remix that is guaranteed to get all eyes in the park looking at you is to IcePick, then drop it to a Double Peg Stall. It is difficult, but really shows you are the master of the IcePick.

Secret

Approach the ramp with just enough speed and let the back peg drop on to the coping. Don't slide it over the coping.

TOOTH PICK

The name makes no sense whatsoever, but the trick is wicked cool.

Step 1

Approach the ramp straight on and as you reach the top, jump.

Common Problem

The back wheel always swings around on me and I have to put my foot down.

You are over-rotating the bike – either you are twisting your hips in Step 2 or the angle of your approach in Step 1 is too big.

Step 2

Push the handlebars down and twist them to lock in, and balance on the front peg over the coping.

Shaun's Tip «

In Step 2 lock your arms as you push the handlebars down and lock in the front peg.

Step 3

Lift the handlebars up and using your shoulder and head rotate the frame around and ride down the ramp.

Remix

This is wicked impressive. Carve up the ramp at a 45 degree angle and do a Tooth Pick Grind. Everything else is the same, but the approach is at a bigger angle and you go faster. This is definitely a trick that attracts the right sort of attention. Try it and you'll see.

Secret

Try to keep the back wheel as high as you can when you push the handlebars down in Step 2, as this helps you balance.

NO FOOTER

When Shaun was growing up a local rider did No Footers all the time. Shaun was captivated by how this trick was so different to anything anyone else could do.

Step 1

Go up the ramp with enough speed to get some air and then jump.

Step 2

While in the air take both feet off the pedals.

Shaun's Tip «

In Step 2 push your feet outwards not upwards. It looks better and means your knees won't hit the handlebars.

Common Problem

I have no brakes on my bike and my pedals always spin in Step 2. What can I do?

Your pedals spin in Step 2 because your feet come off them at different times. Focus on both feet coming off the pedals at the same time and you will be OK.

Step 3

Put your feet back on the pedals and land.

Remix

An awesome remix is the Superman No Footer. In Step 2 kick your feet behind you, not to the side. It looks amazing, because it is amazing.

Secret

Before your feet leave the pedals in Step 2 put your back brakes on so the pedals stay in the same position for the landing.

CAN CAN

Shaun still remembers how scary it was to put his foot over the frame for the first time, even after all these years.

Step 1

Go up the ramp with enough speed to get some air and jump.

Step 2

Level the bike out by pushing the handlebars forward and lift one foot off the pedals and over the frame of the bike to the other side.

Common Problem

I always clip the frame when bringing my foot back.

Shaun has done this many times and it is not good. He solved it by focusing on lifting his foot over the frame, instead of thinking he was bringing it back to the pedal.

Step 3

Lift the foot back over the frame to the pedal and land.

Remix

A simply stunning remix is the No Foot Can Can where both feet point away from the bike. That is even scarier the first time you try it, but well worth the fright.

Secret

You can lift either foot over the frame, but its always easier to lift the front one over as this foot will be closer to the top of the frame.

Shaun's Tip ‹‹

Keep your foot high so it doesn't get caught up on the frame in Step 3 – if you don't the landing will be spectacular for all the wrong reasons.

TAIL WHIP (AIR)

This makes everyone stop to watch. A classic trick that no one looks away from.

Step 1

Go up the ramp, with plenty of speed as you need to be in the air a while, and jump.

Step 2

Kick the frame sideways so that it spins a full 360 around the handlebars.

Common Problem

I can never get the frame to spin the full 360 and I always land next to the bike.

In Step 2 it is very important that you keep your body close to the handlebars so the frame spins around you as well.

Step 3

Catch the pedals as the frame comes back around and land the bike.

Remix

A super hard remix is the One Handed Tail Whip. You do everything the same, but you hold on to the handlebars with only one hand.

Secret

Keep the pedals level and kick the frame sideways with the foot on the back pedal. It makes it easier.

Shaun's Tip «

Have your foot on the outside edge of the pedal in Step 2, so it is easier to kick the frame sideways.

TABLE TOP

As far as Shaun is concerned you can spin your bike, twist your bike, loop your bike as much as you want, but a Table Top is still the most elegant trick in BMX Freestyle.

Step 1

Approach the ramp at a slight angle at a fast speed, and jump.

Shaun's Tip ‹‹

Use your hips to bring the frame up and make it parallel to the floor.

Step 2

Twist the handlebars at 90 degrees to the floor and bring the frame up so it is parallel with the floor.

Common Problem

I'm a bit unsure about doing a Table Top on a ramp and I struggle to do it on a jump box.

Although it doesn't look it, a Table Top is easier on a ramp. On a jump box you really need to twist hard with your hips to get the frame parallel in Step 2.

Step 3

Untwist the handlebars and bring the bike back down to land.

Remix

One of the reasons this trick is a favorite of Shaun's is that it is so good it hasn't changed over the years. If you want to be a top freestyler you must be able to Table Top both to the left and the right.

Secret

To make a Table Top look even better, really turn your highest knee into the frame in Step 2. It adds even more elegance to this great trick.

BAR SPIN

This is a real "hold your breath" trick for the crowd watching, as it looks like the rider doesn't have time to sort out the handlebars before they come back down.

Step 1

Go up the ramp with enough speed to get some air, and jump.

Step 2
Spin the handlebars 360 degrees.

Common Problem
The front end of the bike drops and it wrecks my landing.

In Step 2 squeeze your knees together on the saddle or your legs on the frame to keep the front wheel up when you spin the handlebars.

Step 3

Catch the handlebars and land the bike.

Remix

A fabulous way to make the crowd think it has gone wrong is to land with the handlebars backward. So in Step 2, spin 180 or 540 degrees and then land it. Always gets a good reaction.

Secret

When learning, instead of spinning the handlebars in Step 2 use one hand to guide them 360 degrees. In the 80s this was called a Bus Driver.

Shaun's Tip <<

In Step 3 try to catch the handlebars as they go 270 degrees and don't wait for them to go all the way through to 360 degrees, in case you miss it the first time.

NO HANDER

Shaun learned No Handers in a massive foam pit and before he had it locked he remembers he landed head-first and heard every bone in his body creak and crack. He decided not to ride for the rest of the day. Good decision Shaun.

Step 1

Go up the ramp with enough speed to get some air, and jump.

Step 2

Pull the handlebars into your hips and then let go of them and stretch your arms out wide.

Common Problem

My front wheel always drops and I feel the bike is slipping away from me.

You need to really lock those handlebars to your hips in Step 2 to support the bike when you let go.

Step 3

Grab back hold of the handlebars and land the bike.

Remix

Most freestylers like to spread their arms as much as possible in Step 2, but a cheeky remix is to put both hands behind your head as if you are relaxing in the air. Looks good, but you have to land it.

Secret

Build up your No Hander gradually and at the start just barely let go of the handlebars until you get your confidence.

Shaun's Tip ◄◄

Keep the front wheel high and remember to bring the handlebars to your hips, not the other way around.

TURNDOWN

This is a totally killer trick, because the bike and your body twist in the air so much. Throw in a big jump and you have something special. Well worth learning.

Step 1

Go up the ramp with enough speed to get some air, and jump.

Step 2

While keeping the front wheel up twist the handlebars a full 180 degrees.

Shaun's Tip

Whichever foot is your back foot shows the way you twist the handlebars – if your right foot is your back foot, then you twist the handlebars to the right. Doing this means your knee is out of the way when you twist.

Step 3

Untwist the handlebars and land the bike.

Remix

A top remix is to do a LookBack which looks as spectacular as the TurnDown, but this time the bike is level when you twist the handlebars.

Secret

Turn your knee away from the twist, but keep your leg straight so that the handlebar doesn't get caught behind your knee.

Common Problem

I never have enough room to twist 180 without hitting my legs.

Is your front wheel too low, or is your knee in the way when you are bending your legs? It is one of these two problems.

TOBOGGAN

Whenever Shaun thinks about Toboggans he remembers the time he saw Robbie Morales, BMX legend, throw down a Toboggan on a dirt track. He had the front end so low it just burned the image into Shaun's memory.

Step 1

Go up the ramp with enough speed to get some air, then jump and let go of the handlebars with one hand.

Step 2

Turn the handlebars 90 degrees and with your free hand grab the saddle.

Shaun's Tip ◄◄

Lean back which will help steady the bike and get you out of the way of the saddle.

Step 3

Put your hand back on the handlebars and land the bike.

Remix

A freaky looking remix is a Toboggan One Footed. It looks like you have lost the bike in the air as you only have one hand on the handlebars and one foot on the pedals, but you really have the bike under total control.

Secret

Do the trick early in your jump to get the most out of your air time.

Common Problem

I can never grab the saddle and hold it.

Sounds like you are doing a seat touch more than a Toboggan. Either start the trick earlier or get more air in your jumps.

BACK FLIP

This is the show stopper. This is the one that makes everybody gasp.

Step 1

Go straight up the ramp at a good fast pace and as the front wheel goes over the coping tilt your head back and arch your body.

Shaun's Tip ◀◀

Only practice over water. You do not want to find out you cannot do this over concrete.

Step 2

As the back wheel goes over the coping push the back pedals forward to help with the rotation.

Step 3

As you do the flip, spot where you are going to land and land the bike.

Remix

As this is such a stunning trick there are a whole variety of remixes. Shaun likes the Back Flip No Hander, but you can also Back Flip Table Top, One Hander, One Footer, Tail Whip – the list goes on, and all of these are stellar.

Secret

Everything needs to be smooth, so don't jerk your head back or pull hard on the handlebars. Smooth is the key.

Common Problem

I never get all the way round and face plant in the water.

This is because you are not committing to the trick. You need to keep your head back to get the full rotation.

FLAIR

This trick is simply mind blowing. Try explaining it to someone who has never seen it as the bike does all sorts of crazy rotations. The best way is to describe it is a Back Flip with a Twist.

Step 1

Approach the ramp fast and at an angle.

Step 2

As your front wheel goes over the coping, tilt your head back like in a Back Flip, but this time over the shoulder that is lower on the ramp, as this is the way you will twist.

Shaun's Tip «

You must have your Back Flips locked before trying a Flair.

Common Problem

My back wheel always hits the coping as I try to land.

You have the Back Flip but not the twist. Try dropping the lower shoulder more in Step 2 to tuck into the twist.